Water Sports
Adventure

T0066368

Rob Waring, *Series Editor*

HEINLE
CENGAGE Learning

Australia • Brazil • Japan • Korea • Mexico • Singapore • Spain • United Kingdom • United States

Words to Know

This story is set in the United States (U.S.). It happens in the Columbia River Gorge, in the states of Oregon and Washington.

(A) Water Sports. Read the paragraph. Then, write the number of the correct <u>underlined</u> word next to each item in the picture.

Water sports are usually very fast and fun! In <u>water-skiing</u> **(1)**, a person stands on one or two thin skis and a very fast <u>boat</u> **(2)** pulls the skier over the water. In <u>wakeboarding</u> **(3)**, a person stands on a special wide board and a boat pulls them along the water. In <u>kiteboarding</u> **(4)**, a person stands on the same kind of board, but a large kite pulls them. All of these activities can be very enjoyable—especially if the <u>waves</u> **(5)** on the water are big!

kite

Water Sports

board

B An Unusual Inventor. Read the paragraph. Then, match each word with the correct definition.

This story is about water sports in the Columbia River Gorge. A gorge is an area between two mountains, so there is usually a lot of wind there. Cory Roeseler [reɪslər] lives in the area, and he loves new things and adventure! Roeseler is a mechanical engineer who likes to invent new things. He likes to design new sports equipment that uses the power of the wind.

1. gorge _____

2. wind _____

3. adventure _____

4. mechanical engineer _____

5. invent _____

6. design _____

7. equipment _____

a. a narrow place between two high areas

b. new and different experiences

c. a natural, fast movement of air

d. someone who studies how machines work

e. make or draw plans for something

f. things used for a particular activity or purpose

g. create something that has never been made before

skis

It's a cold winter day in the Columbia River Gorge. "[I] can't believe what blue sky we've got today! It's beautiful," says Cory Roeseler as he prepares his equipment. It may not be warm, but for Roeseler, the wind makes it a perfect day.

To most people, the very cold wind would feel uncomfortable. However, it gives Roeseler a different feeling. He says, "[It] feels like power … feel some wind!" He then adds, "It's going to be good today." But good for what? Roeseler puts on a special suit for water sports. He then starts to carry a big kite down to the water. "Okay, let's go **sailing**,"[1] he says with a smile.

_____

[1] **sail:** move with the power of the wind, usually with a cloth called a 'sail'

🎧 CD 3, Track 03

You see, Cory Roeseler doesn't just fly kites on windy winter days. Roeseler flies with them! Thirty-year-old Roeseler was one of the first people to really experience the sport of kiteboarding. He uses a kite to catch the power of the wind. This wind power has helped Roeseler to do new and interesting things. It's been especially helpful in developing new adventure sports, like kiteboarding.

But what is kiteboarding like? How does it feel? According to Roeseler, "It's sort of a **rolly**,[2] **wavy**,[3] free feeling ... where you know at any moment, you can just **launch**[4] off the water for a few seconds and fly."

---

[2]**rolly:** *(slang)* move from side to side because of wind or waves
[3]**wavy:** *(slang)* move up and down because of wind or waves
[4]**launch:** go up into the air quickly

And that's exactly what Roeseler does! As the kite pulls him quickly along, he lifts himself out of the water and launches into the air. That may be why the young mechanical engineer compares kiteboarding to the way birds fly. He says that the power of the wind in a kite can be like a bird moving its **wings**.[5] The lifting power, or 'lift,' of both things can **overcome gravity**.[6] This lift allows them both to 'fly'.

---

[5]**wing:** part of a bird's body that is moved to fly
[6]**overcome gravity:** become stronger than the natural force that pulls things to Earth

The power of the wind in a kite is like the lift of a bird's wings.

Wind power is something that's easily found in the gorge which divides Washington and Oregon. That makes the Columbia River Gorge one of the best places in the world to kiteboard. However, for inventor Cory Roeseler, the gorge is more than just a place to have fun; it's a place where he can test his new inventions.

Roeseler has always loved water sports. When he was a teenager, he was the first person to 'test pilot,' or try out, the sport of kite-skiing. Usually, people water-ski behind a boat. However, Roeseler decided to use wind power to ski behind a kite. It worked! Later, he became a mechanical engineer. Then, in the 1990s, he invented and designed a lot of water sports equipment. Eventually, he became famous in the area of water sports.

Sequence the Events

What is the correct order of the events? Write numbers.

_____ invented water sports equipment

_____ became famous

_____ was a test pilot for kite-skiing

_____ became mechanical engineer

Now, Roeseler is ready to test his newest invention for playing with the wind. To do this, Roeseler has asked his friends for some help. He takes the group to the water to show them his invention. It's a new kind of wakeboarding boat that has a sail on the back. Roeseler explains how the sail works. "The sail's going to **stabilize**[7] us so we don't **tip over**,"[8] he says excitedly.

However, his friends don't seem as certain. Roeseler's friend Jeff, who will be testing the invention, is watching **nervously**[9] nearby. "Why are you nervous?" someone asks. "I've never seen anything else like that before," he says, laughing. "So it's a little **freaky**,"[10] he explains. But what makes Roeseler's boat so different?

---

[7]**stabilize:** keep in place; stop sudden changes
[8]**tip over:** fall to the side
[9]**nervous:** worried about a future event
[10]**freaky:** unusual in an unpleasant or unexpected way

In recent years, more and more people have started using towers for wakeboarding. A tower is a structure that is put on a wakeboarding boat. It allows people to place the wakeboarding rope higher. This higher rope gives more lift to the wakeboarder and makes it easier to jump in the air. It's also easier on the wakeboarder's body.

Roeseler's design is similar to that of other wakeboarding boats. However, his tower is 17 feet off the water. That's six feet higher than other wakeboarding boats. The higher rope will allow the wakeboarder to jump even higher than before! Roeseler has also added a sail to the tower. The sail will stabilize the tower and the wake boarder when the boat is moving.

1 foot = 0.31 meters

wakeboarding rope

tower

sail

Roeseler's New Invention

Jeff jumps into the water and the boat starts to move. As the boat goes faster, he is able to stand up on his wakeboard. He then starts moving quickly and easily across the water. After a few moments, he speeds up, goes towards a wave, and launches high into the air. The new invention works! Everyone is very happy. "Nice!" says Jeff as he gets back in the boat. "It works," he says with surprise. "It's **nuts**.[11] I didn't think it would!"

And how does Roeseler feel about the apparent success of his invention? "I'm a little more **confident**[12] ... but, we'll see. It's got to go on a big wakeboard boat and get tested in the right environment," he explains.

---

[11] **nuts:** crazy or not normal; not expected
[12] **confident:** certain of one's abilities

For Cory Roeseler, the right environment seems to be the Columbia River Gorge. For him it's the right place to live, and the right place to find adventure with his new water sports.

According to Roeseler, life sometimes seems almost too good to be true. For him and his friends, living in the area is so wonderful that it's like being in a **dream**.[13] He adds that they're also happy that they're not going to wake up and find that it's gone. It's seems like Roeseler and his friends want every day to be a water sports adventure!

---

[13] **dream:** events and images experienced in the mind while sleeping

Infer Meaning

1. How does Cory Roeseler feel about the Columbia River Gorge?

2. What does he mean by 'it's like being in a dream'?

After You Read

1. On page 4, how does Cory Roeseler feel about the wind?
   A. uncomfortable
   B. happy
   C. unsure
   D. nervous

2. In paragraph 1 on page 7, the word 'experience' means:
   A. fly
   B. use
   C. do
   D. be

3. How does the kite help Roeseler?
   A. It catches the wind and provides lift.
   B. He uses it to pull his boat.
   C. It keeps him warm.
   D. It reduces his speed.

4. Kiteboarding feels _____ flying.
   A. just
   B. about
   C. way
   D. like

5. Which is NOT a good heading for page 10?
   A. Inventor Tests Inventions in Gorge
   B. Kiteboarders Like Windy Area
   C. River Gorge Wind Too Strong
   D. Fun at River Gorge

6. When Roeseler started kite-skiing, he was:
   A. under ten years old
   B. 12 years old
   C. between 13 and 19 years old
   D. thirty years old

7. In paragraph 1 on page 12, 'it' refers to:
   A. a new invention
   B. the wind
   C. a kite
   D. a wakeboard

8. According to page 12, what do Roeseler's friends think about the new wakeboarding boat?
   A. They think it's great.
   B. They think it will work well.
   C. They are not sure about it.
   D. They really don't like it.

9. What's new about Roeseler's wakeboard boat?
   A. It has a tower.
   B. It has a rope.
   C. It's a smaller boat.
   D. It has a higher tower than other boats.

10. In paragraph 2 on page 14, the word 'allow' means:
   A. gives
   B. lets
   C. makes
   D. agrees

11. Roeseler thinks his latest invention:
   A. needs more testing
   B. is nuts
   C. is unbelievable
   D. works perfectly

12. Why can every day be a perfect day for Roeseler?
   A. He can kiteboard every day of the year.
   B. He loves where he lives and what he does.
   C. The weather is usually windy in the gorge.
   D. all of the above

My Water-Skiing Adventure

June 12

Well, this is it.... I'm taking my first water-skiing lesson tomorrow morning. I'm a little nervous, but it'll be an adventure!

June 13

I met my teacher early this morning. Before we started, he said I had to practice on dry land. First, he asked me to sit down on the ground. Then he gave me the 'tow rope,' the line that will connect me to the boat. While he held the rope, I had to stand up only using the power in my legs. It wasn't easy. I'm just not used to doing that! He also told me to remember one important thing—I must drop the tow rope immediately if I fall over.

Then the fun really began. We put the equipment into the boat and went out into deep water. My teacher said that he would start the boat slowly and then go faster. My job was to stand up when the boat was going quickly. It sounded easy. But as soon as I stood up, I tipped over. Then, I forgot to drop the rope! I went flying through the water and my skis came off. I felt really silly and we had to start again. I tried this twenty-five times, but I could not stand up. Water-skiing is harder than I expected.

Water-skiing is hard work but fun!

June 14

Today things were a little better. After five attempts, I was able to stand up. I waited until I found my balance on the skis, and then stood up slowly. I was surprised at how hard the water felt under the skis. It was like stone. The wind on my face was really strong. I was water-skiing and it felt wonderful!

June 15

Today was even better than yesterday! There were some big waves and I learned how to move over a wave without falling. Tomorrow I'm going to try it using only one ski—I can't wait!

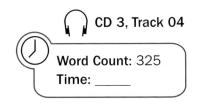

CD 3, Track 04

Word Count: 325
Time: _____

Vocabulary List

adventure (3, 7, 18)
boat (2, 10, 12, 14, 17)
confident (17)
design (3, 10, 14)
dream (18, 19)
equipment (3, 4, 10, 11)
freaky (12)
gorge (2, 3, 4, 10, 18, 19)
invent (3, 10, 11, 12, 15, 17)
kiteboarding (2, 7, 8, 10)
launch (7, 8)
mechanical engineer (3, 8, 10, 11)
nervous (12)
nuts (17)
overcome gravity (8)
rolly (7)
sail (4, 12, 14)
stabilize (12, 14)
tip over (12)
wakeboarding (2, 12, 14, 17)
water-skiing (2, 10)
wave (2, 17)
wavy (7)
wind (3, 4, 7, 8, 9, 10)
wing (8, 9)